When In Rome

Coloring Book

An Italian Adventure for the Whole Family

By Shay Peretz © 2016

ItalyColoringBook@gmail.com

www.Facebook.com/WhenInRomeColoringBook

www.ItalyColoringBook.com

Welcome to Italy

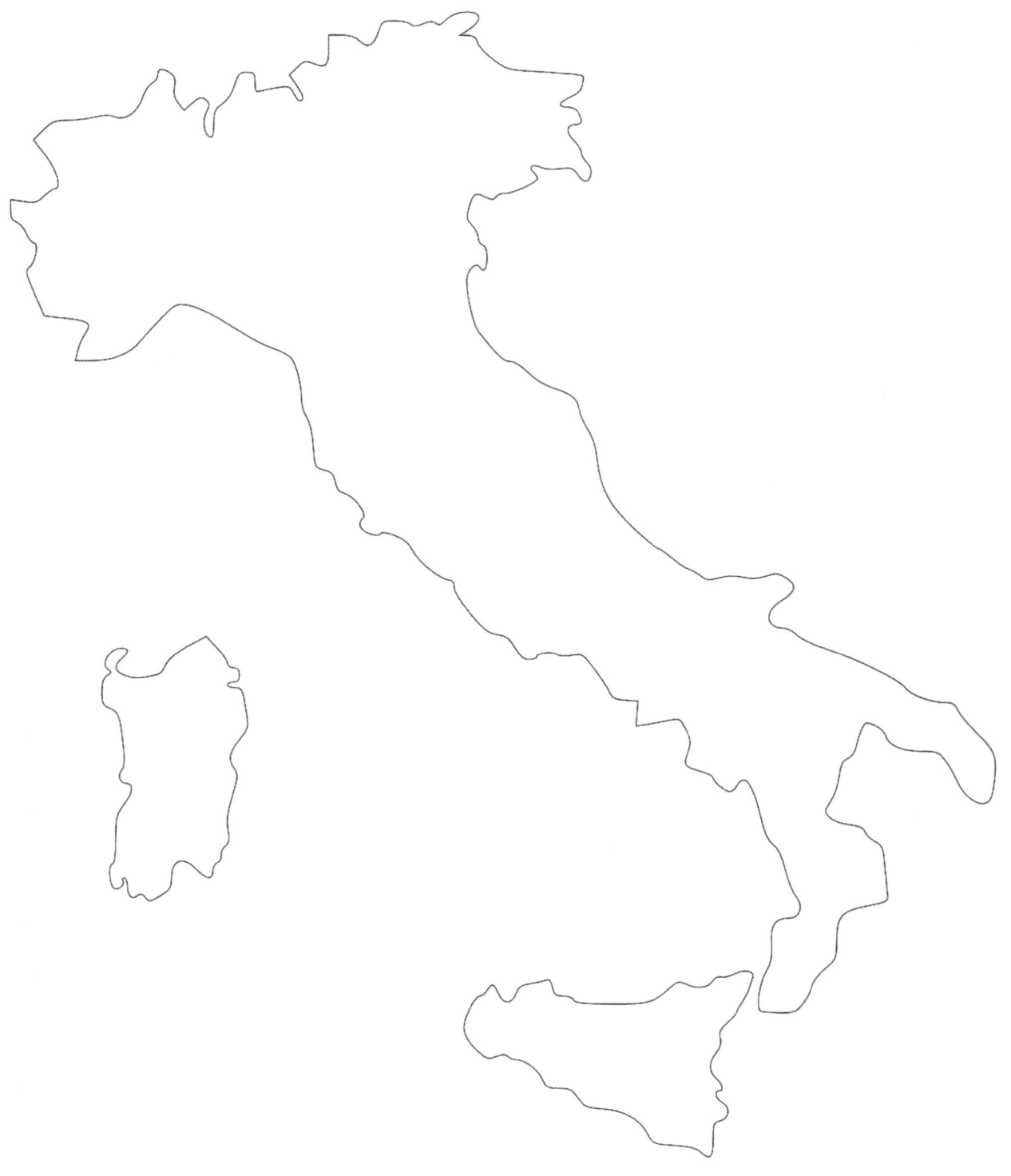

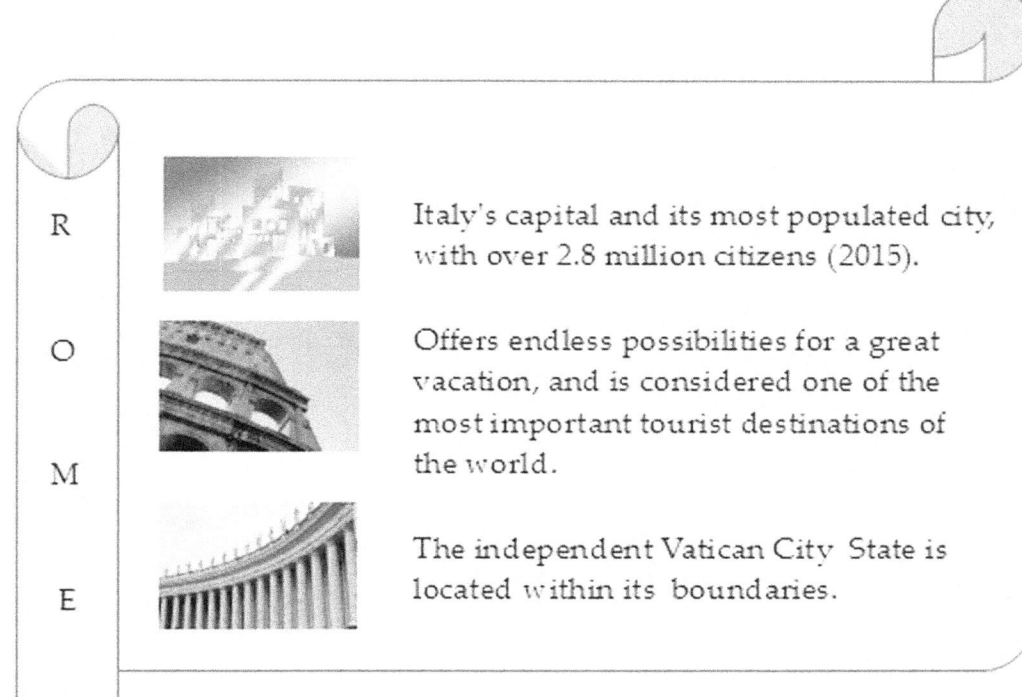

R

O

M

E

Italy's capital and its most populated city, with over 2.8 million citizens (2015).

Offers endless possibilities for a great vacation, and is considered one of the most important tourist destinations of the world.

The independent Vatican City State is located within its boundaries.

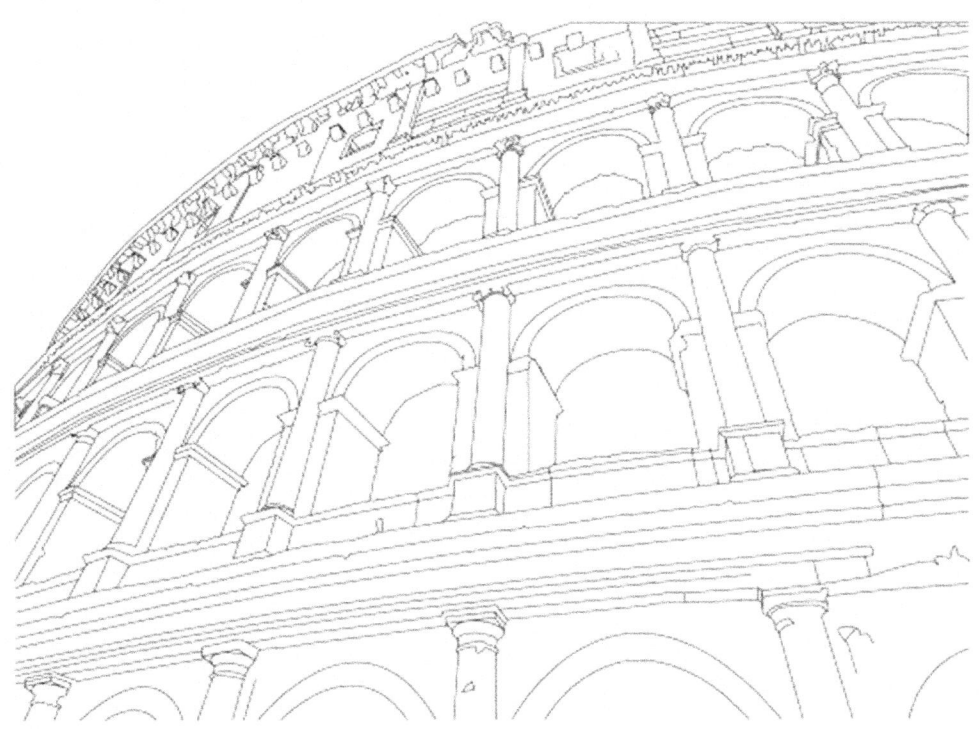

The **Colosseum** *(Colosseo)* in Rome. Also called: The Flavian Amphitheatre *(Anfiteatro Flavio)*. It is the largest amphitheatre ever built.

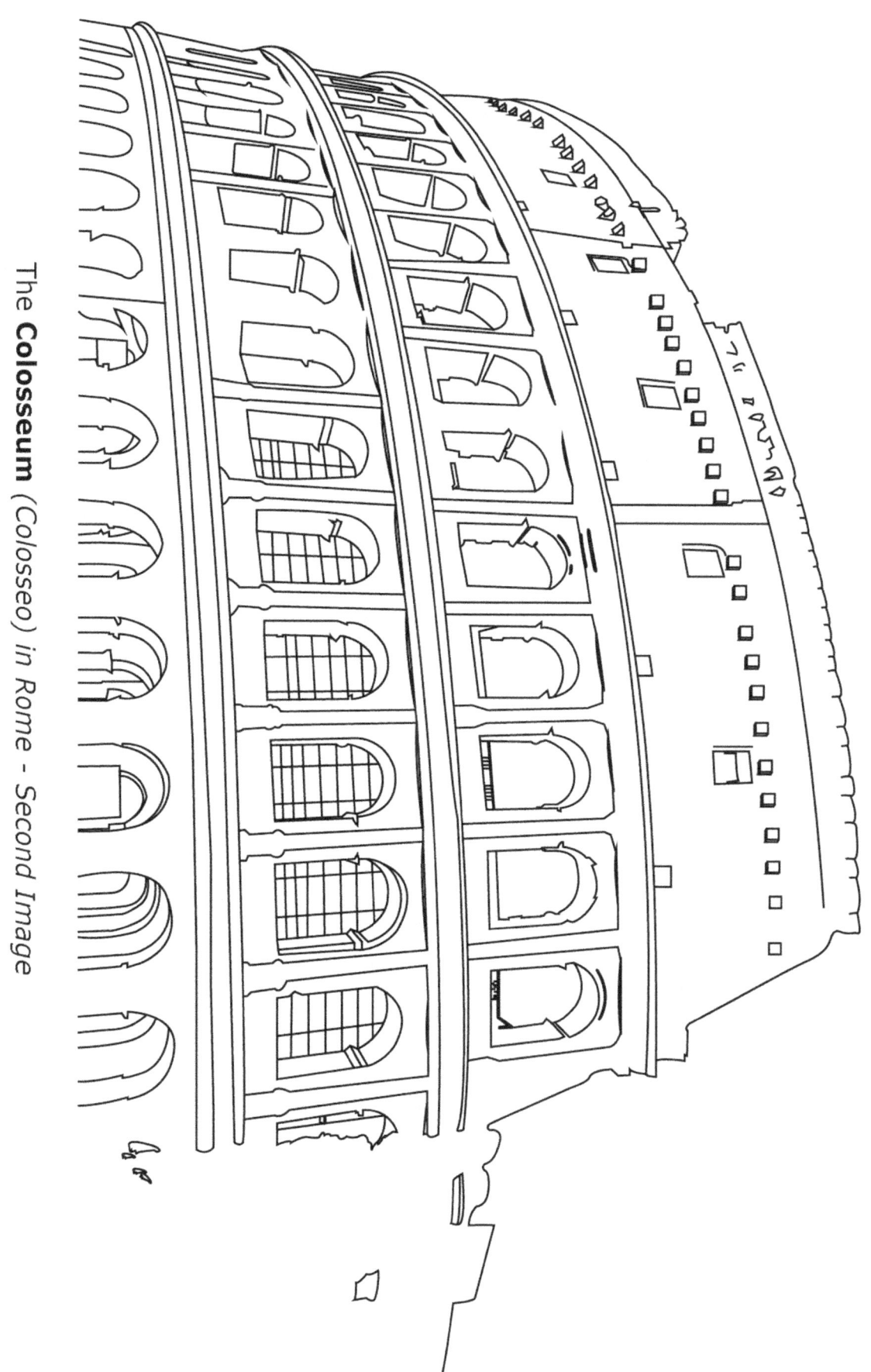

The **Colosseum** (*Colosseo*) *in Rome - Second Image*

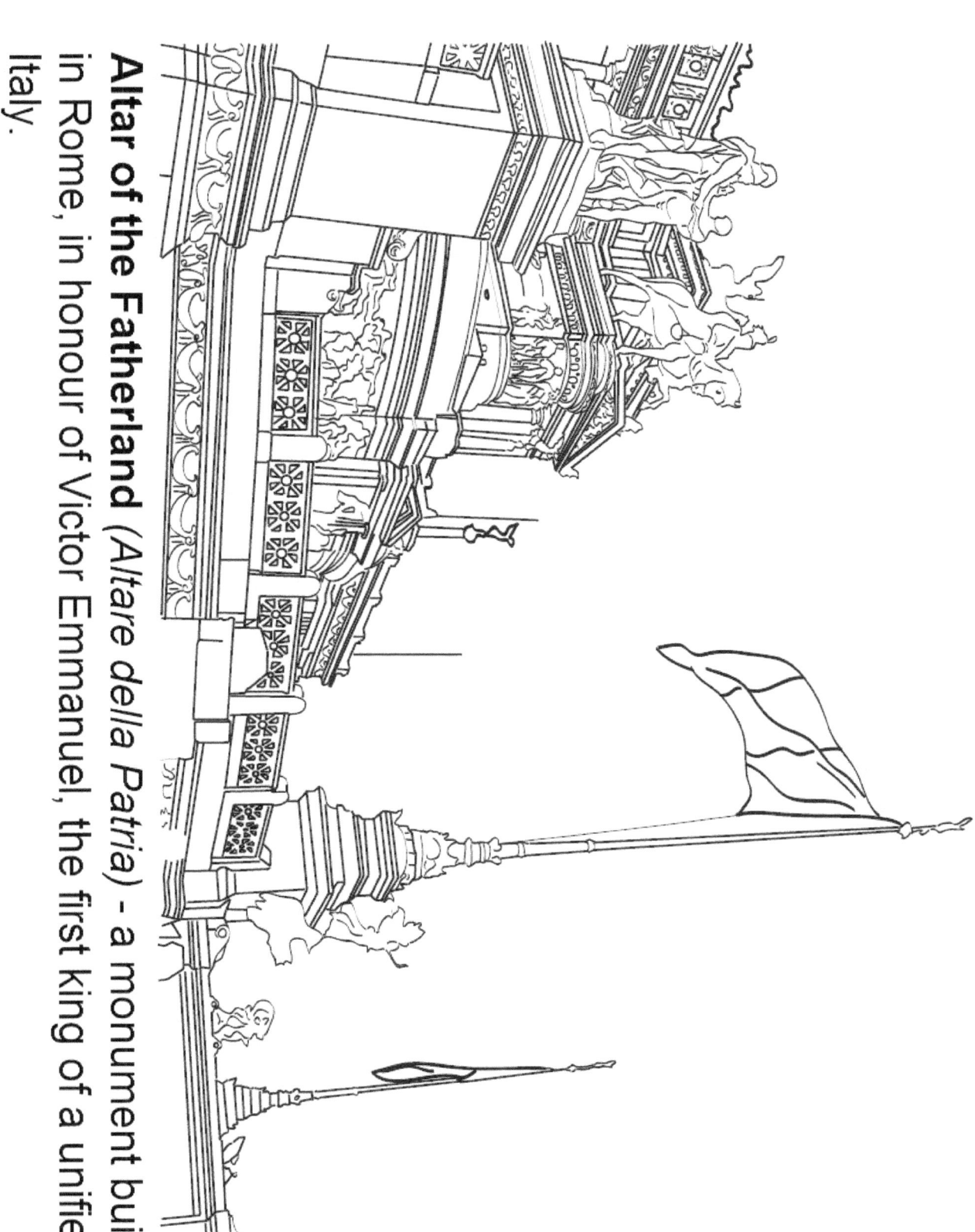

Altar of the Fatherland (*Altare della Patria*) - a monument built in Rome, in honour of Victor Emmanuel, the first king of a unified Italy.

The **Pantheon** in Rome - one of the best preserved Roman temples.

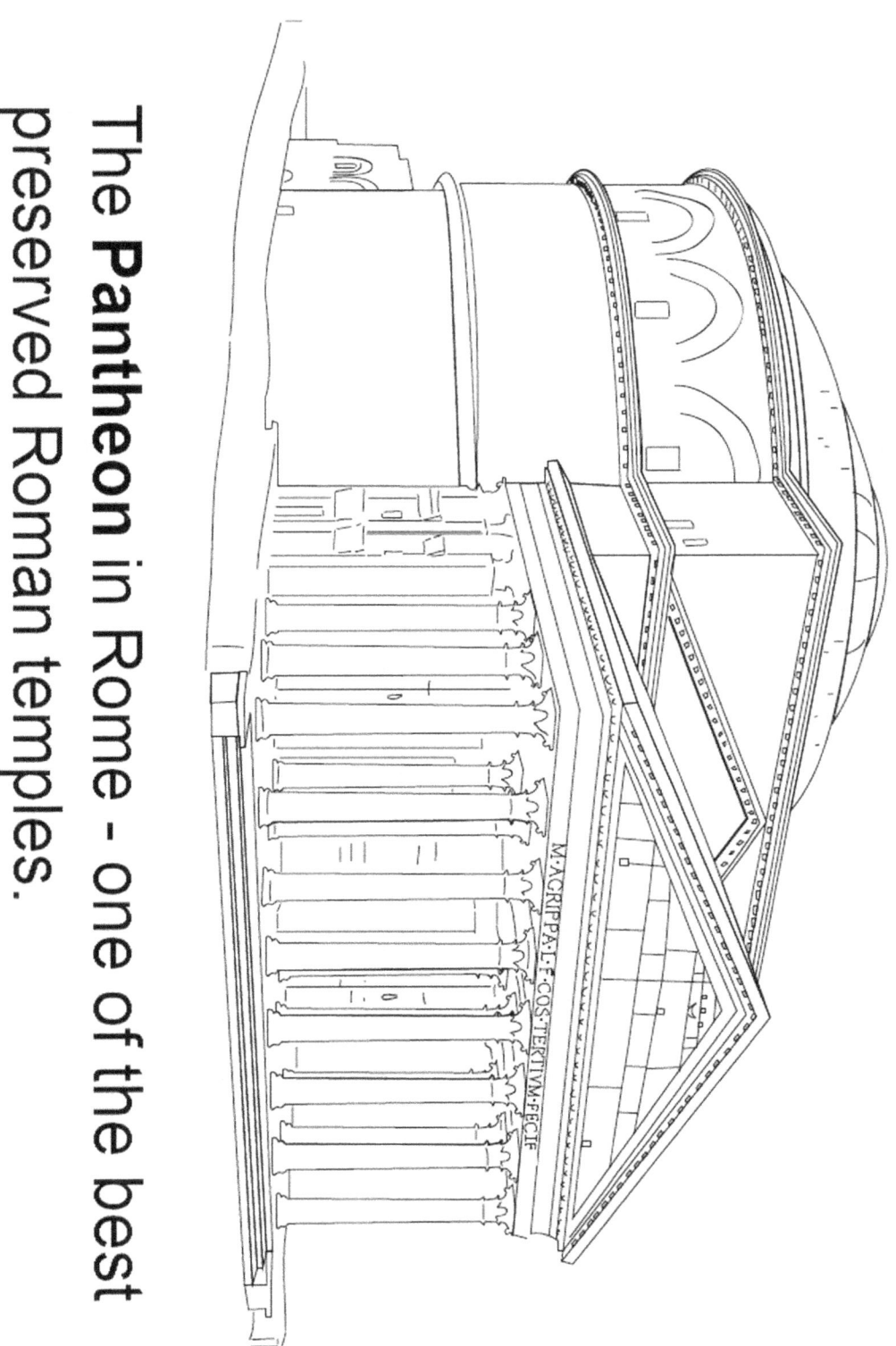

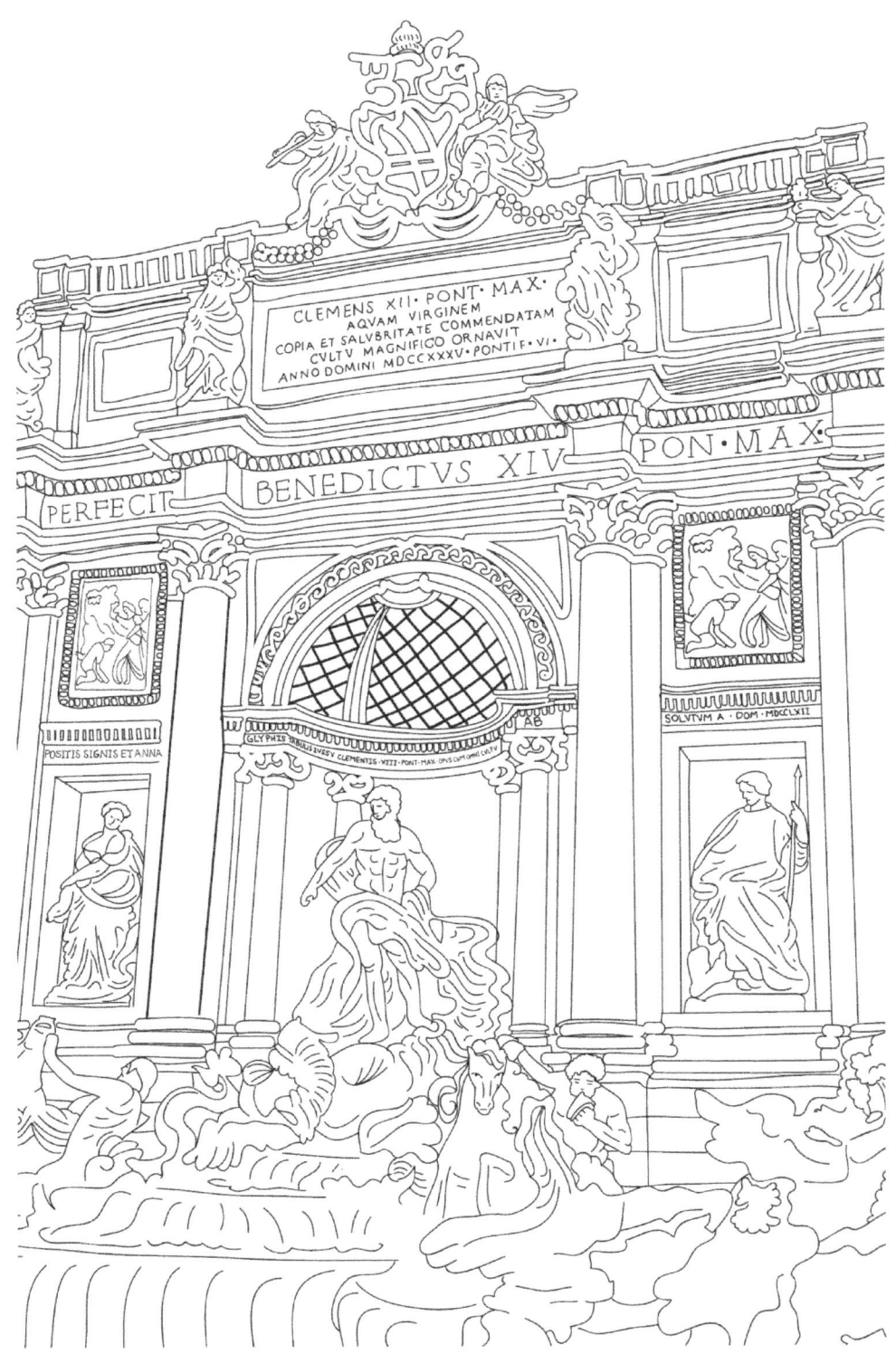

The Trevi Fountain *(Fontana di Trevi)* - the largest Baroque fountain in Rome.

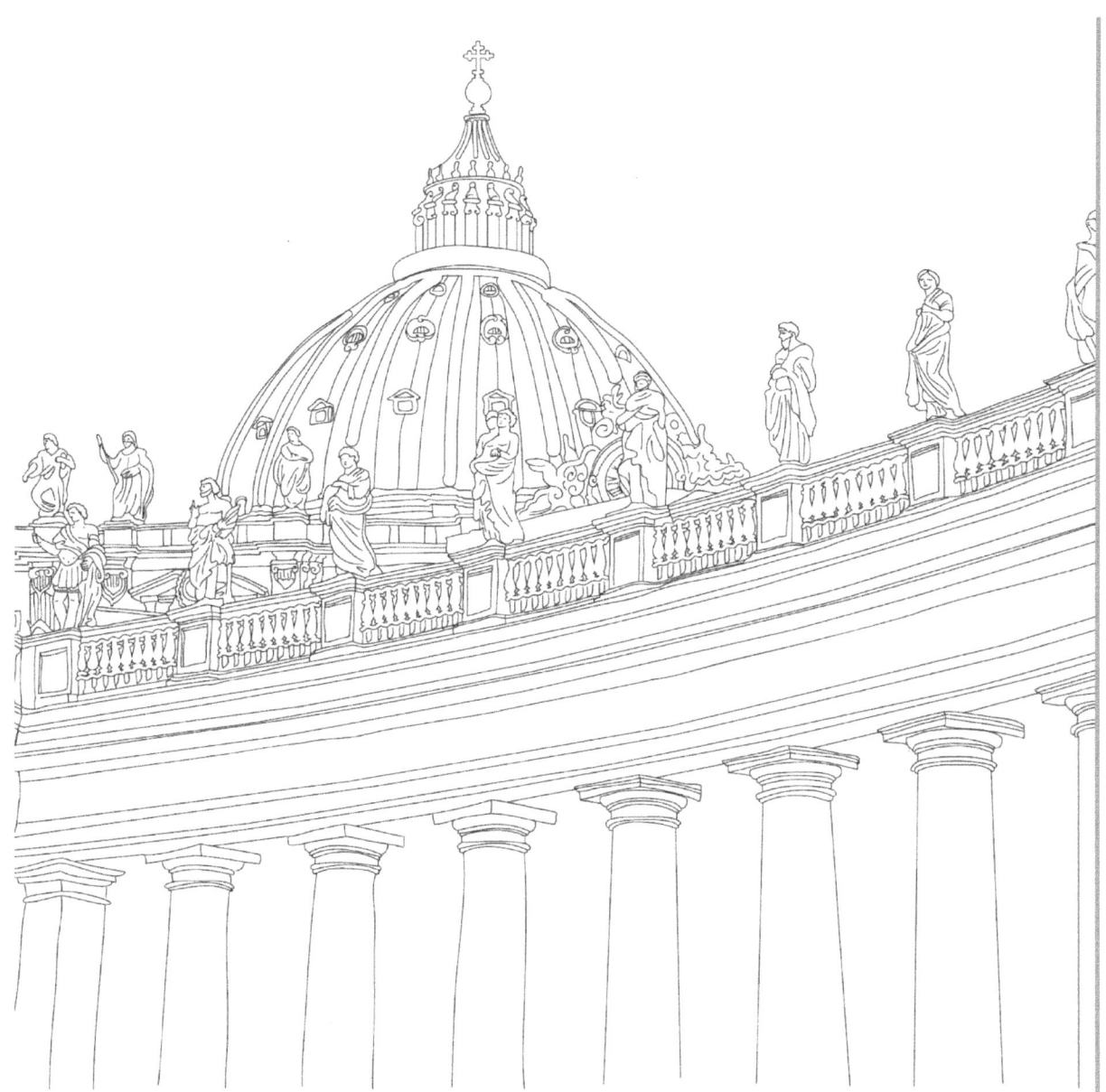

The Papal Basilica of St. Peter in the Vatican *(Basilica Papale di San Pietro in Vaticano)* - an Italian Renaissance church in Vatican City.

Rome – Points of Interest

Italy's capital is the most popular travel destination in Italy, and one of the most visited cities in Europe, as it offers a unique experience of culture, art and archaeology.

Some of the city's main points of interest are hiding in the following word search puzzle. Try to find them.

```
E N A P O E Z S I T A L N N H Z
S S P T A E Z V N U T I A A S E
E M E A V F R O N A A M N E R M
H N U E I I R C M U A O A I E Z
G S P E O E E P M A V E E P M R
R O A R S B S T A A I S M N P R
O T N U I U M L N H A F A A A Z
B M T I R O M A N F O R U M E T
A U H L A T Z N L A A R E E U R
I E E C M Z T H A H M N E N O Z
R S O S A I P N I C O A T F O F
E S N I A T N U O F I V E R T S
L O P S P A N I S H S T E P S N
L L I H E N I L O T I P A C U E
A O O I M A H Z I A P E G V I E
G C N L L U N N A N M L O E S I
```

Capitoline Hill   Colosseum
Galleria Borghese   Pantheon
Piazza Navona   Roman Forum
Spanish Steps   Trevi Fountain
Vatican Museums

17

Pisa

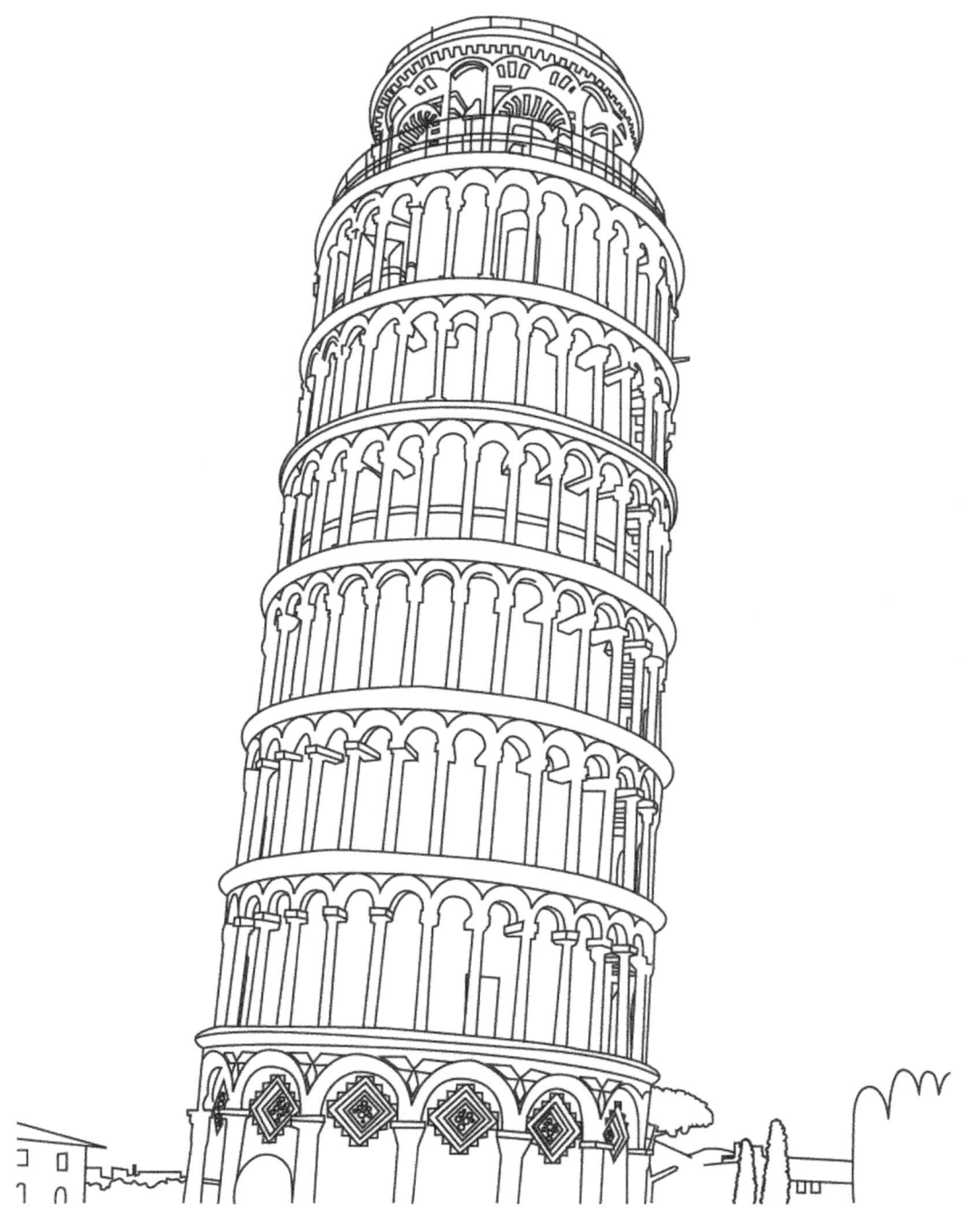

Leaning Tower of Pisa *(Torre pendente di Pisa)* in
Piazza del Duomo, the city of Pisa

Venice

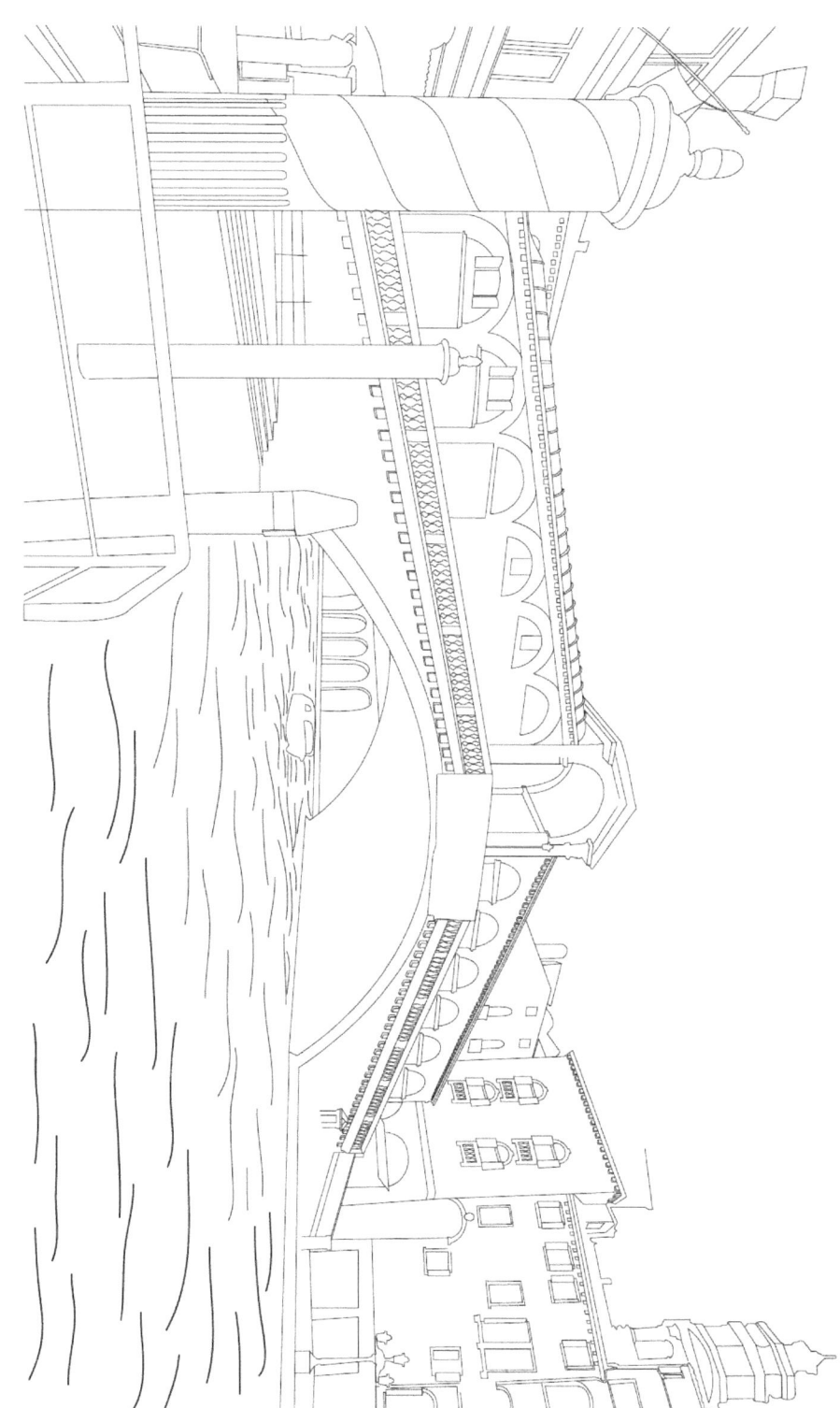

Rialto Bridge (*Ponte di Rialto*), the oldest bridge across the Grand Canal in Venice

Gondolas in Venice

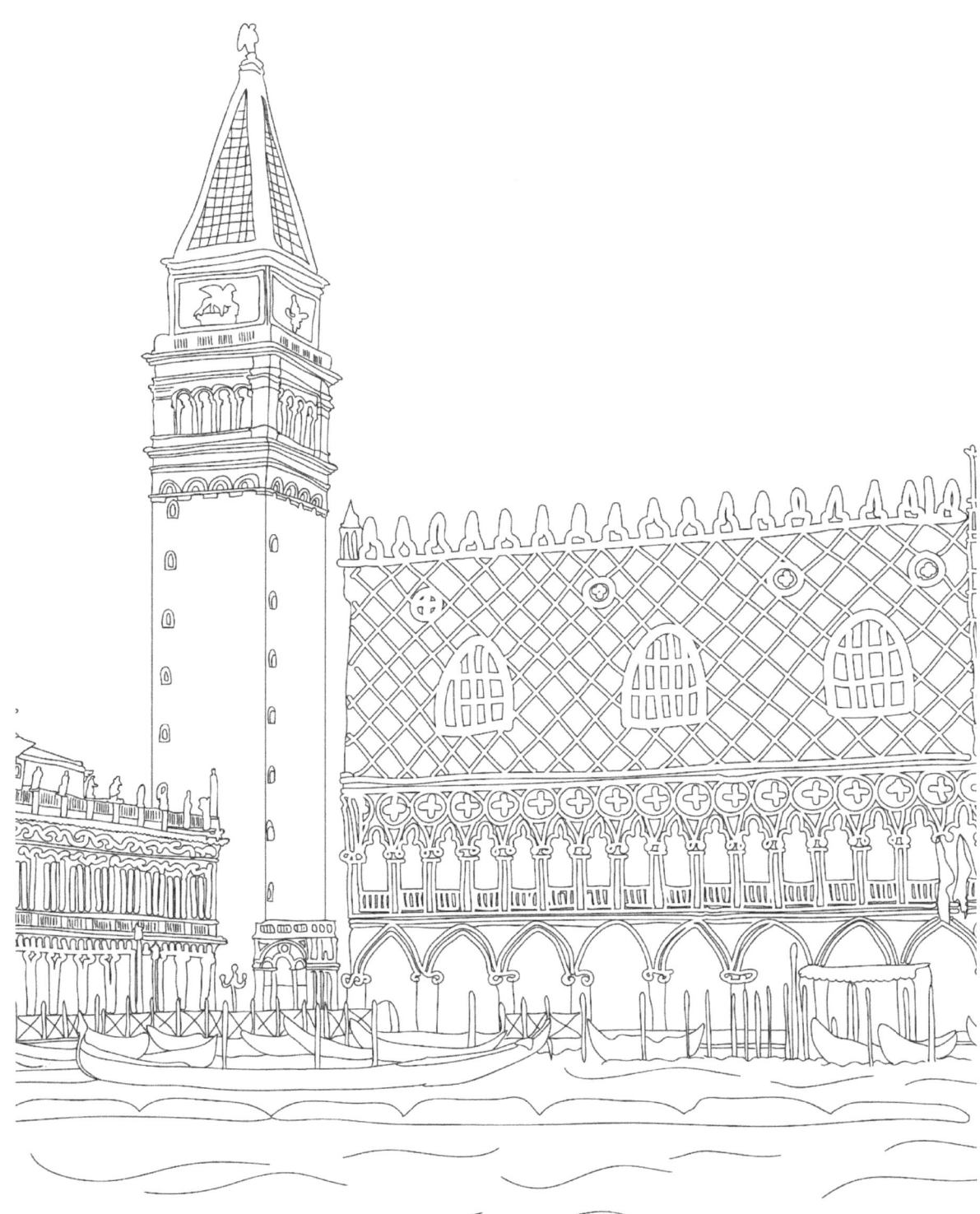

St Mark's Campanile *(Campanile di San Marco)* - the bell tower of Saint Mark's Basilica in Piazza San Marco, Venice.

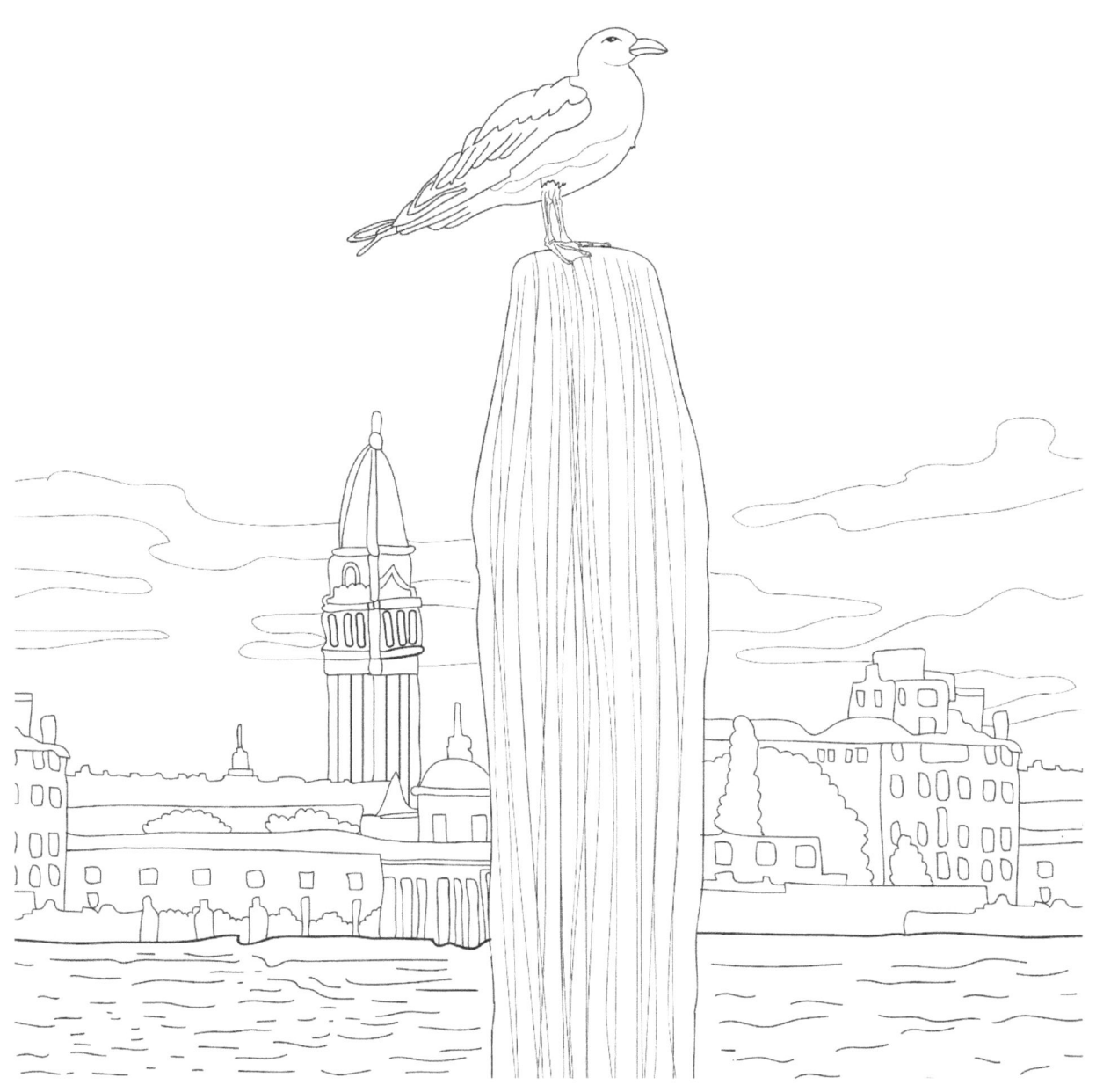

A seagull, Venice in the background.

Burano

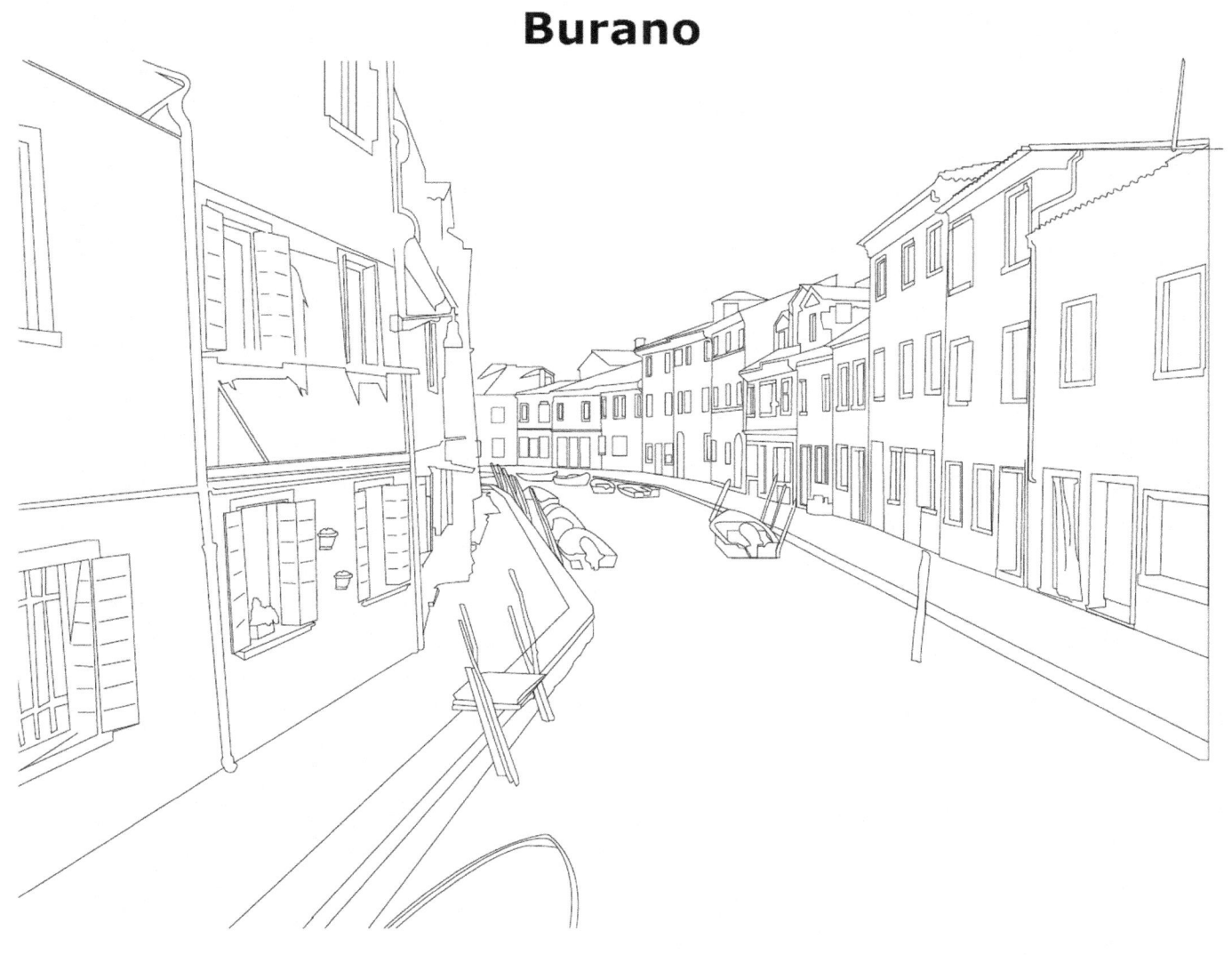

Burano, *the colored island of the Venetian Lagoon*

Florence

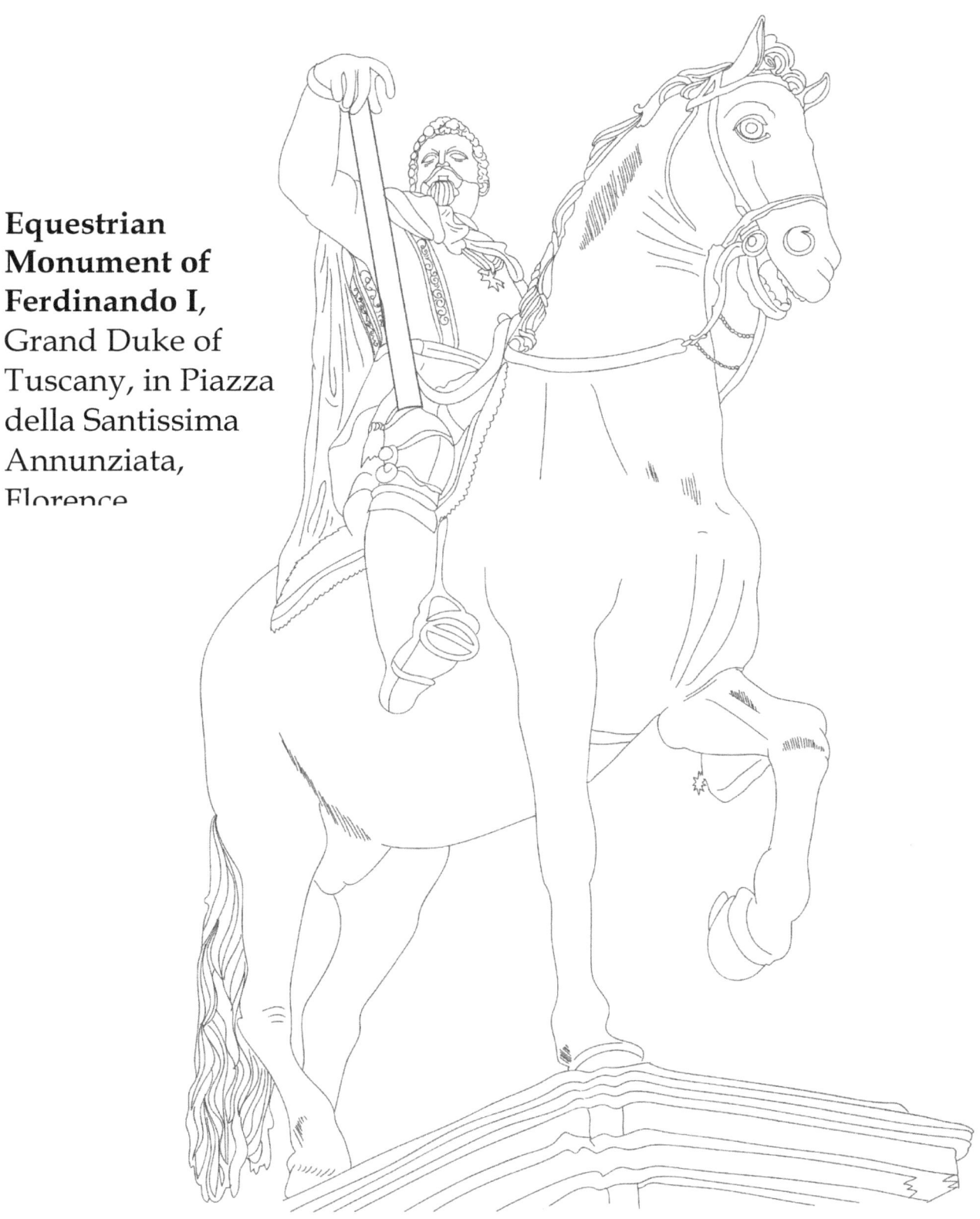

Equestrian Monument of Ferdinando I, Grand Duke of Tuscany, in Piazza della Santissima Annunziata, Florence.

Ponte Vecchio (The Old Bridge) in Florence

Florence Cathedral (*Cattedrale di Santa Maria del Fiore*).

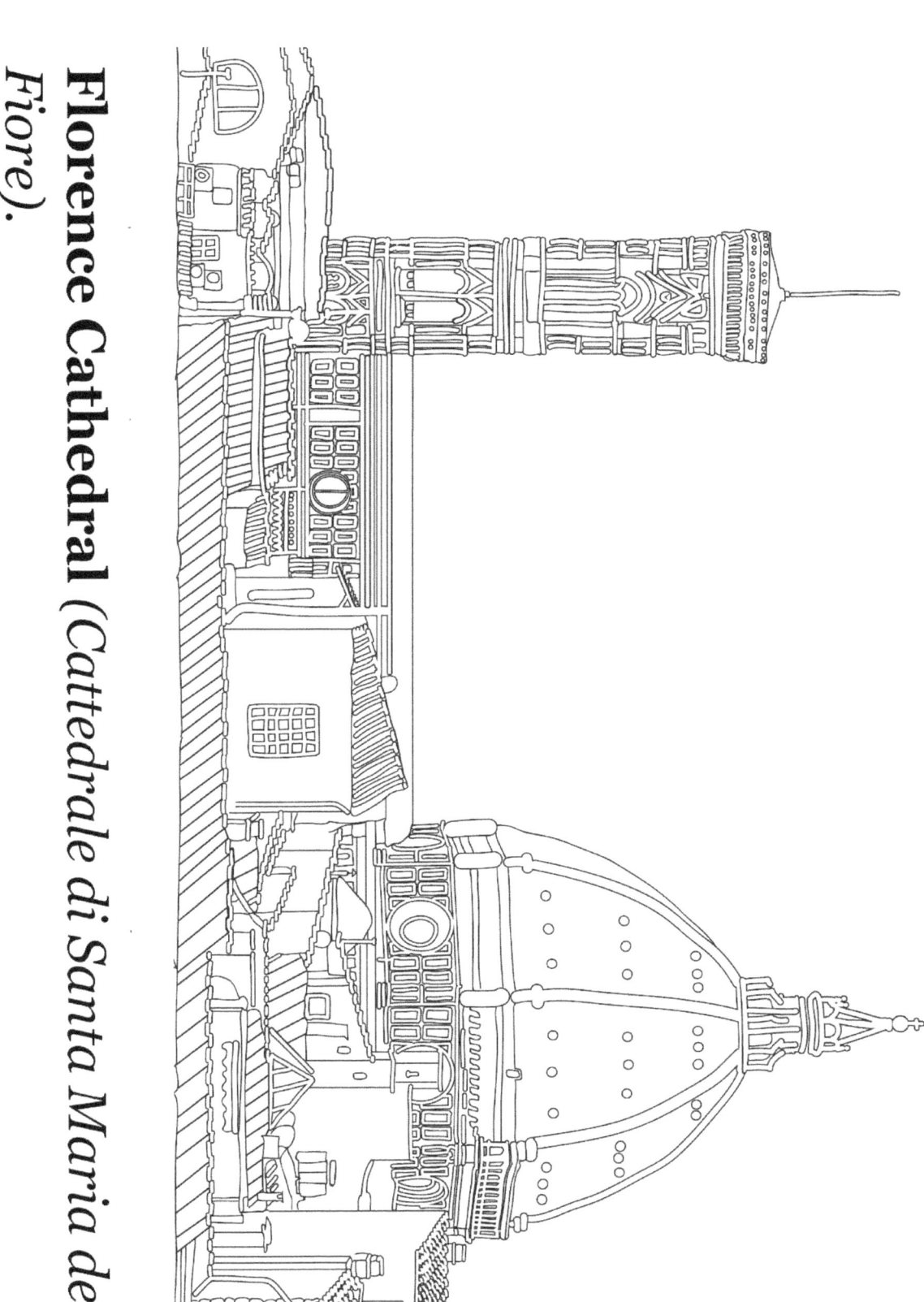

Turin

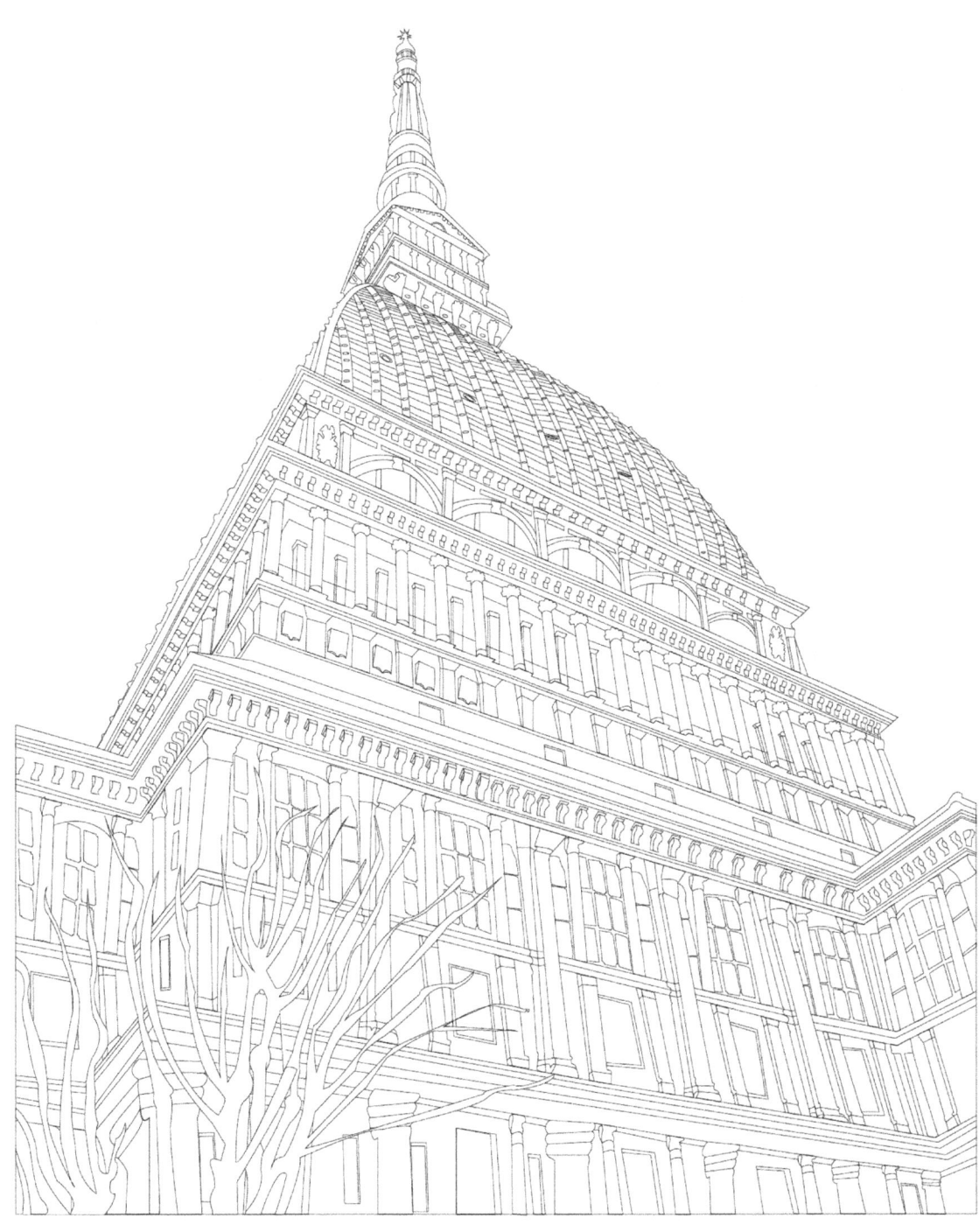

Mole Antonelliana in Turin. It was built by the
Italian architect Alessandro Antonelli.

Catania

Catania Cathedral
(Duomo di Catania, Cattedrale di Sant' Agata) – a Roman Catholic cathedral in Catania, Sicily, dedicated to Saint Agatha.

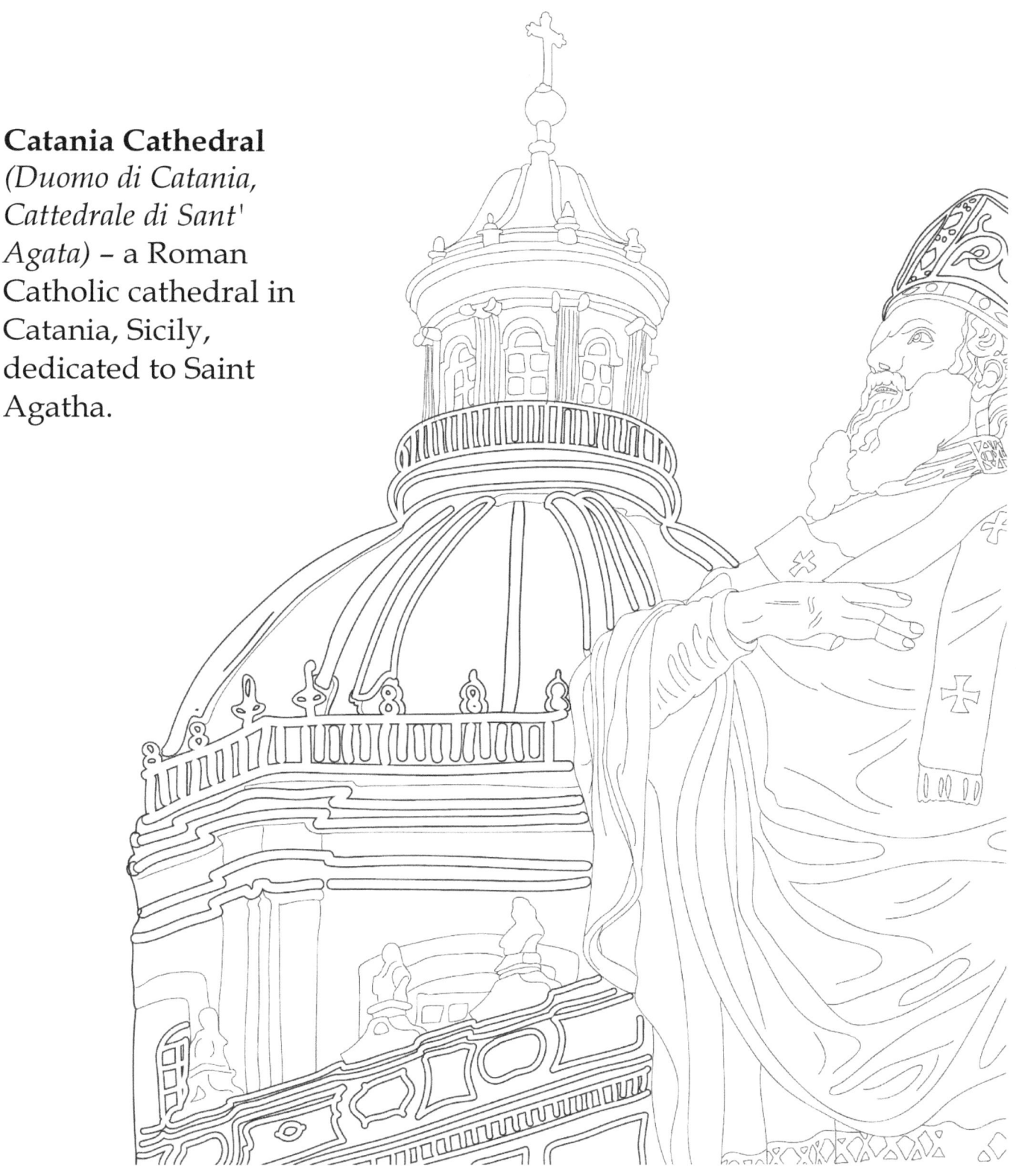

Verona

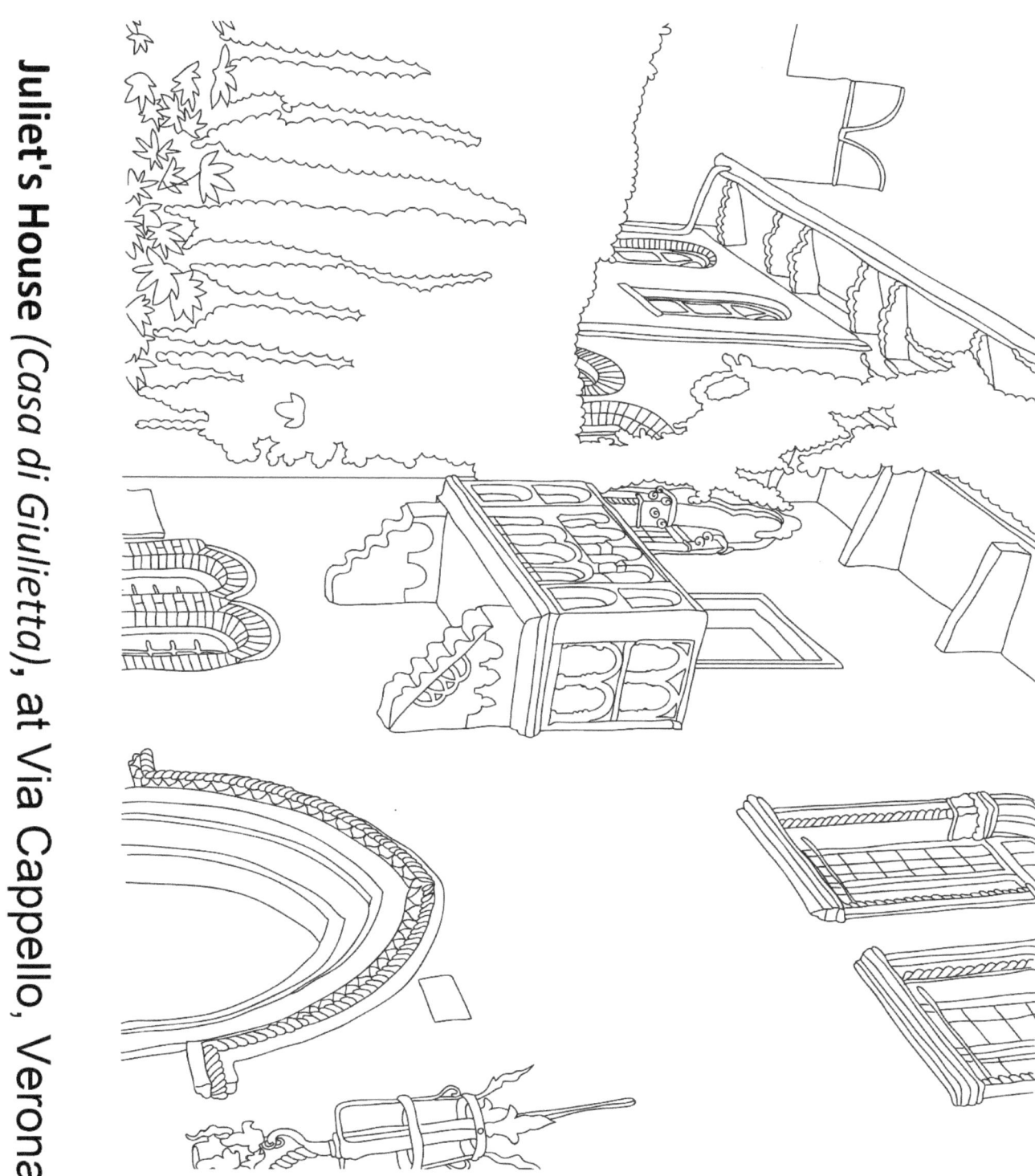

Juliet's House (*Casa di Giulietta*), at Via Cappello, Verona.

The **Verona Arena Arena** (*Arena di Verona*), in Piazza Bra, Verona. It is one of the biggest amphitheatres in the world.

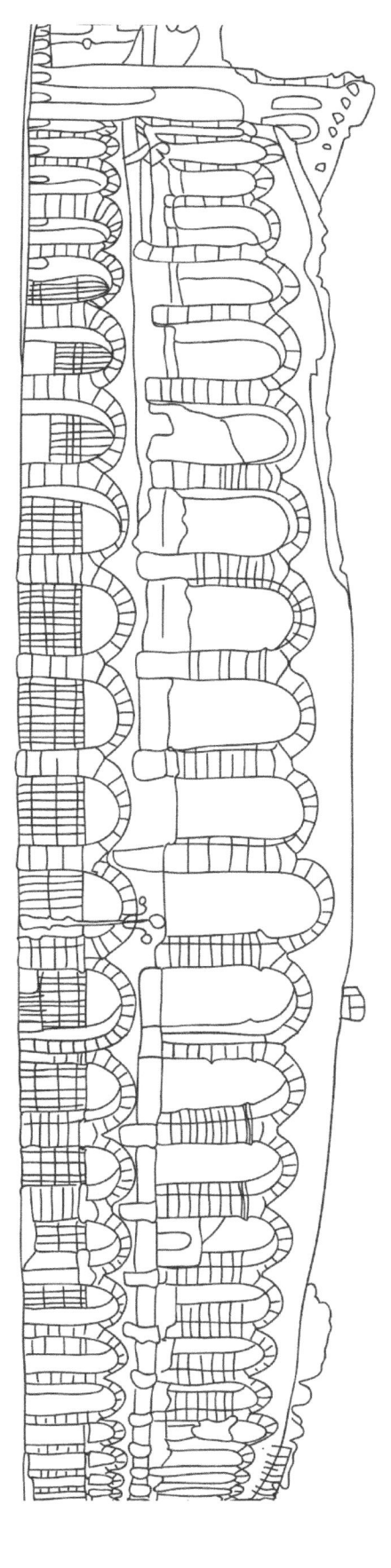

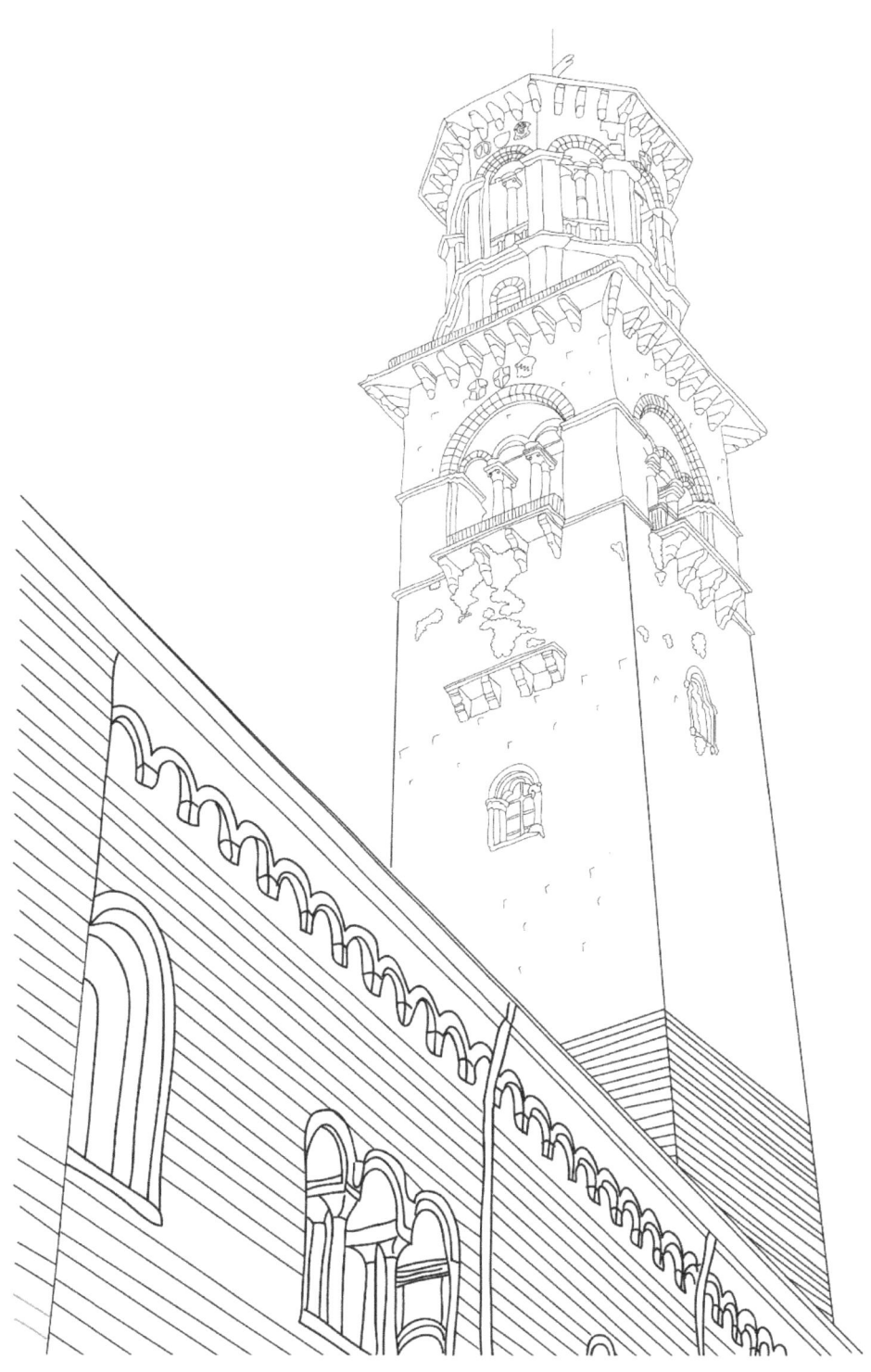

The **Lamberti Tower** *(Torre dei Lamberti)* in Piazza delle Erbe, Verona.

Naples

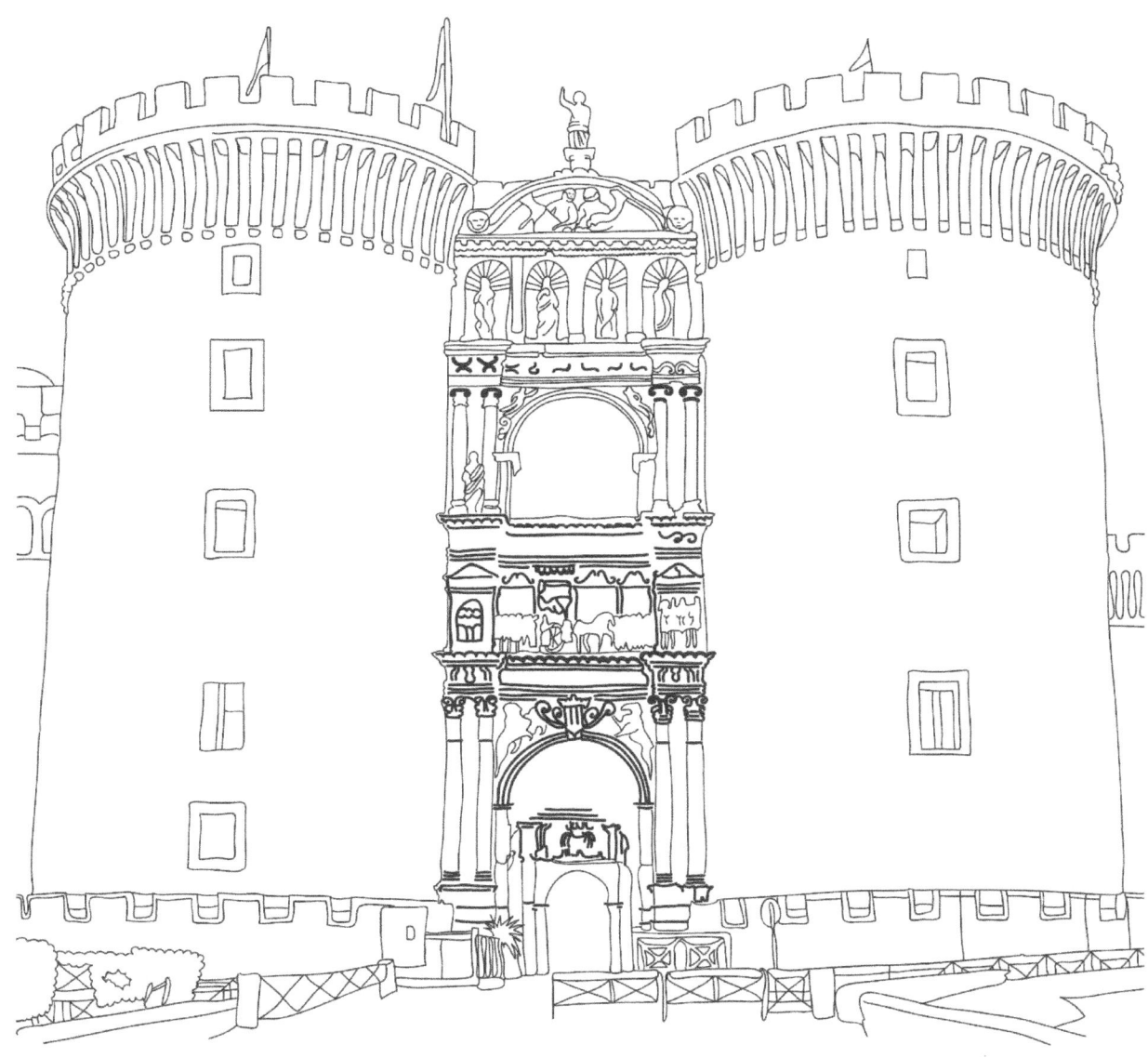

Castel Nuovo *(Maschio Angioino)*, next to Piazza Municipio, Naples.

Milan

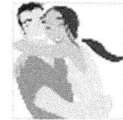
Italy's second most populated city, with over 1.3 million citizens (2015).

One of Europe's main fashion hubs.

Home to many museums, art galleries, and other points of interest.

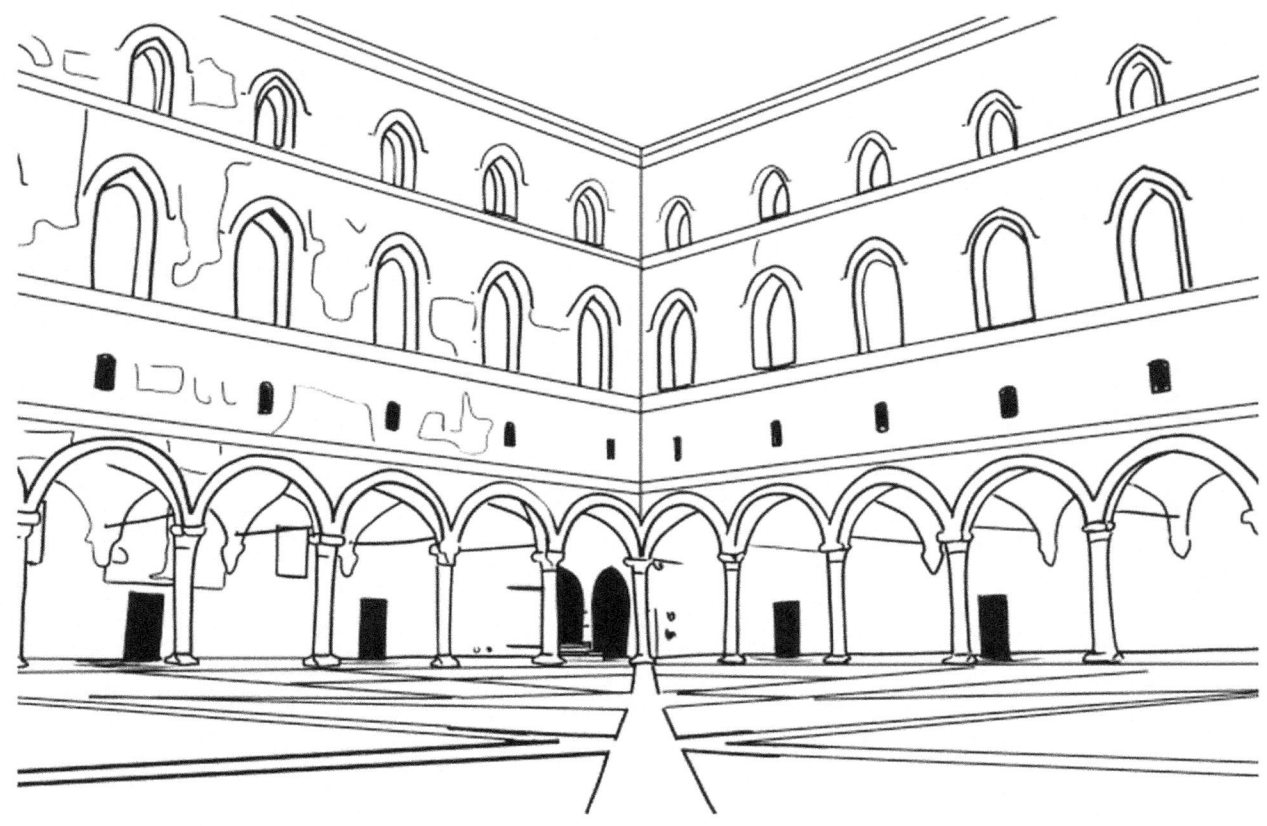

Sforza Castle *(Castello Sforzesco)* in Milan.
The castle was built in the 15th century by
Francesco Sforza, Duke of Milan.

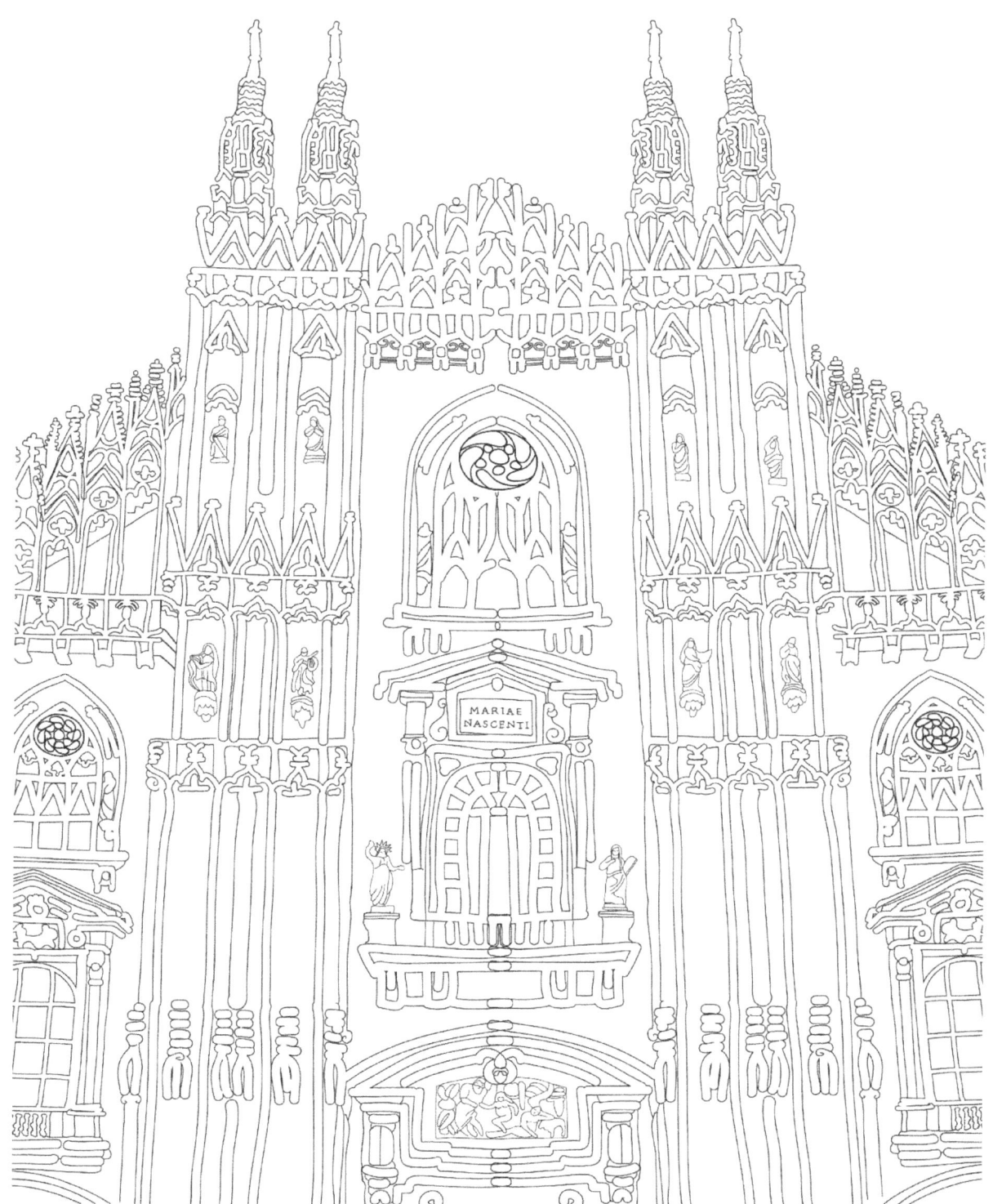

Milan Cathedral *(Duomo di Milano)*, the largest church in Italy. It is the seat of the Archbishop of Milan.

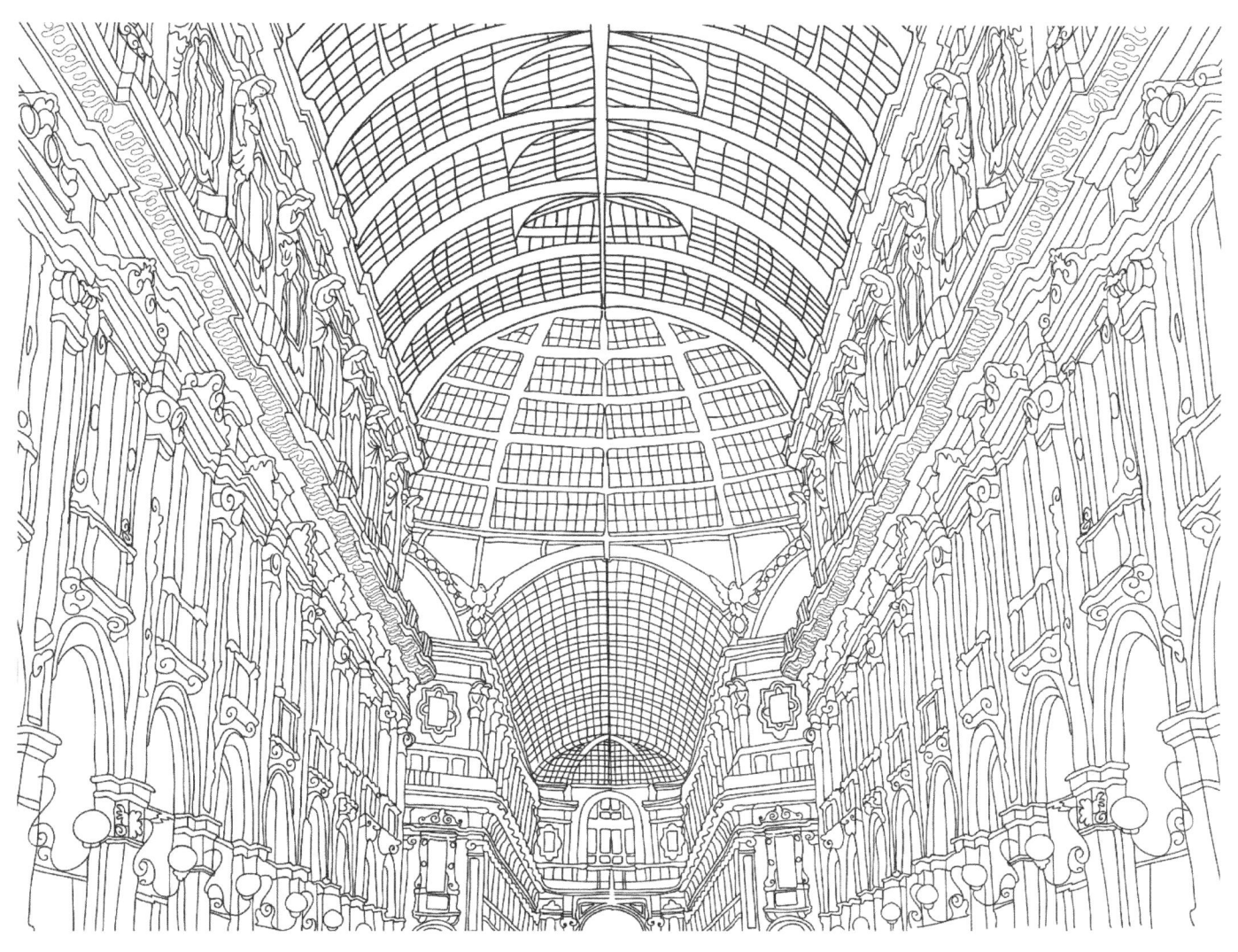

Galleria Vittorio Emanuele II in Milan.

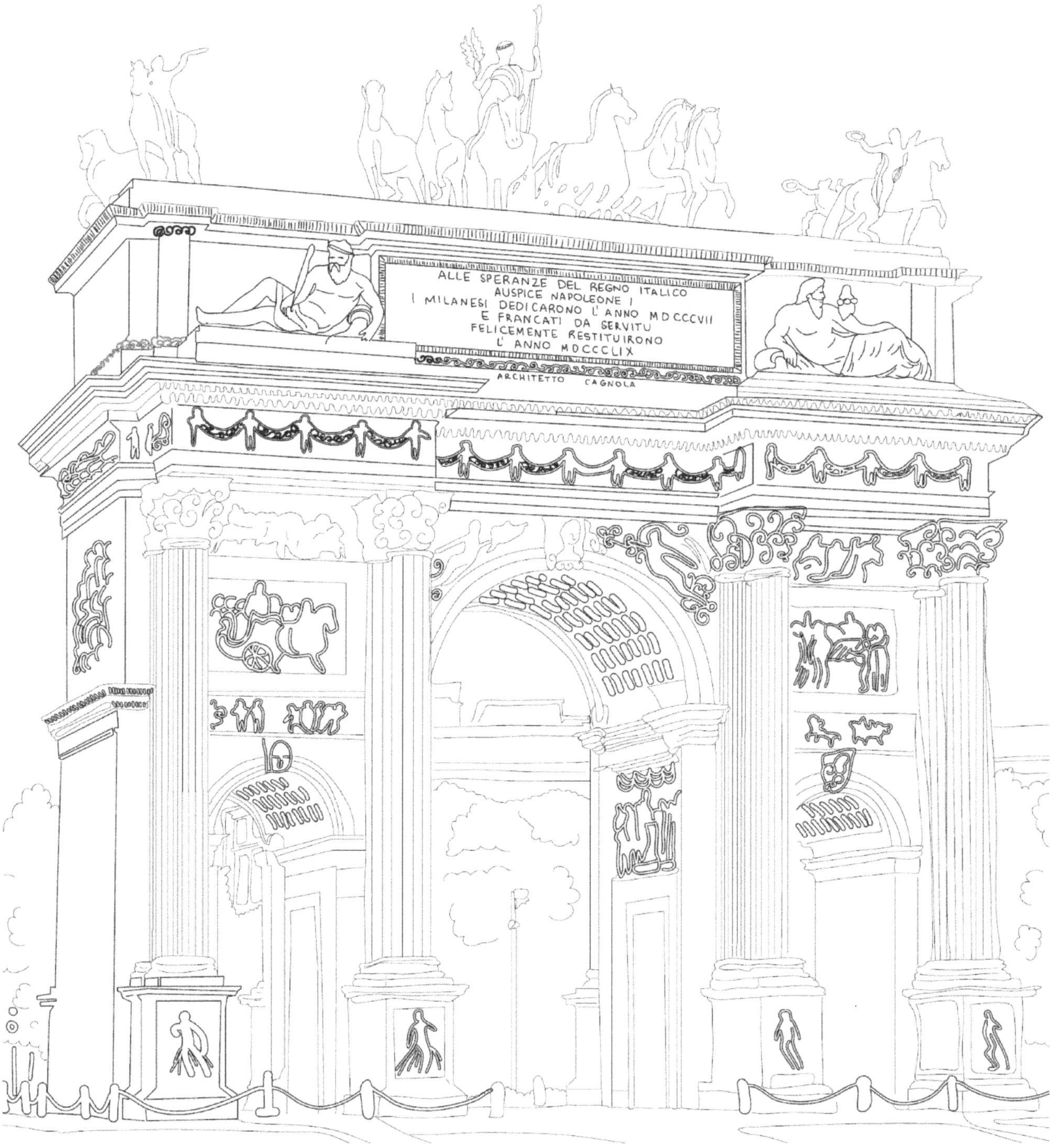
ALLE SPERANZE DEL REGNO ITALICO
AUSPICE NAPOLEONE I
I MILANESI DEDICARONO L'ANNO MDCCCVII
E FRANCATI DA SERVITU
FELICEMENTE RESTITUIRONO
L'ANNO MDCCCLIX
ARCHITETTO CAGNOLA

Arch of Peace *(Arco della Pace)* in Piazza Sempione, Milan.

Milan – Points of Interest

Milan is one of the most popular travel destinations in Europe, and millions of visitors enjoy the city's splendid views and architecture every year.

Some of Milan's most known locations are hiding in the following word search puzzle. Try to find them!

```
A O P S C L V N A A N S D D T T
C R A A L E O O I P T E M F E A
N C A N R T A I A S T Z I I C A
A L F F E C G T L H N L L A I T
R O I E C E E A H A G P A T E M
B P L D N A C I V I C A N E R A
E E R E R N S N V V L E C Z A N
R S E L R P C A L R E E A C T O
R N Z E S E N I C I T A T R O P
O A E A T C A T N I R A H A R T
T S F O R Z A C A S T L E E L C
N S M N W I E I P C S M D R I Z
B P I R E L L I T O W E R I E D
N E F C T G T A E R P R A L N A
P T R E S R T I I C A A L A C S
I N E L C P N A C E A I I F A P
```

Arena Civica   Milan Cathedral   Navigli
Pirelli Tower   Porta Ticinese   San Fedele
San Sepolcro   Sforza Castle   Torre Branca

Crossword

Here is an opportunity to demonstrate what you already know about Italy, and learn some more. Good luck!

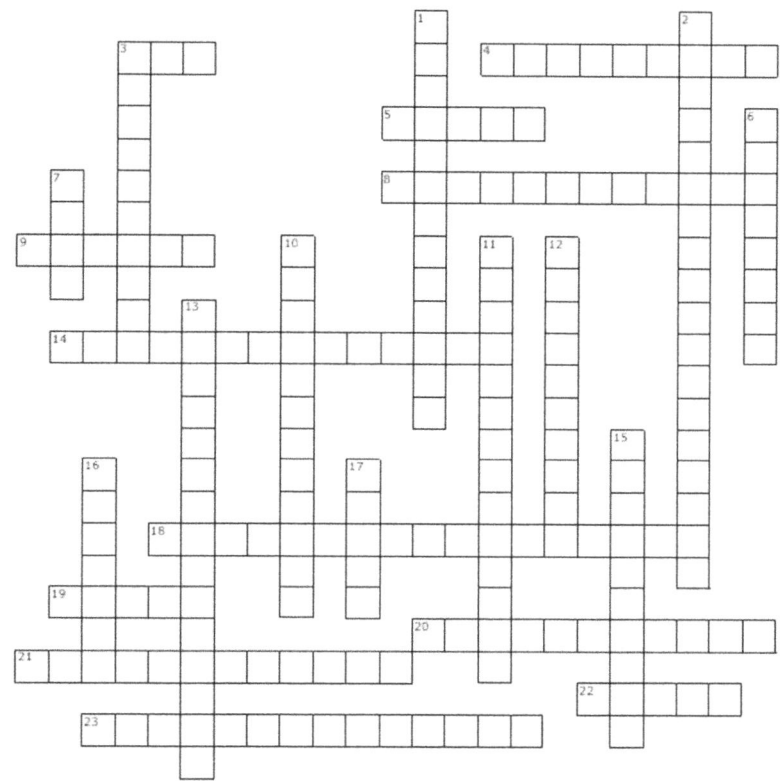

Across

3. Italy's national public broadcasting company
4. Famous amphitheatre in Rome
5. The captial of Lombardy region
8. Italian painter and sculptor during the Renaissance
9. Country in Europe bordering Italy
14. Italian poet during the middle ages
18. Popular daily newspaper in Italy
19. National dish in Italy
20. Trade fair in Milan
21. High speed train in Italy
22. The region of Rome
23. Skyscraper in Milan

Down

1. Art museum in Florence
2. Important culture event in Venice
3. Popular sport in the north of Italy
6. The most popular sport in Italy
7. The capital of Apulia region
10. The most popular religion in Italy
11. Italian Astronomer during the Renaissance
12. Business district in Milan
13. Italian Painter
15. Known Italian football club
16. Famous Italian fashion company
17. The capital of Piedmont region

Maze

Walk through the maze and collect letters on the way. Which Italian historical monument have you come across?

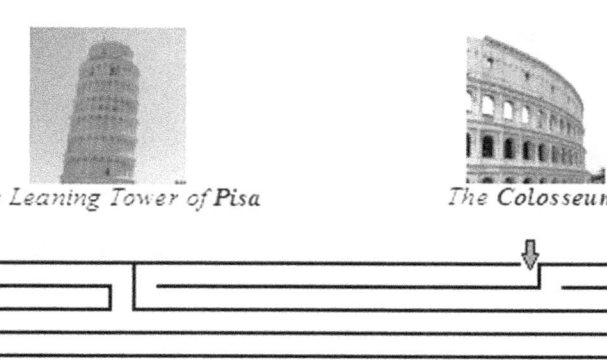

The Leaning Tower of Pisa   The Colosseum

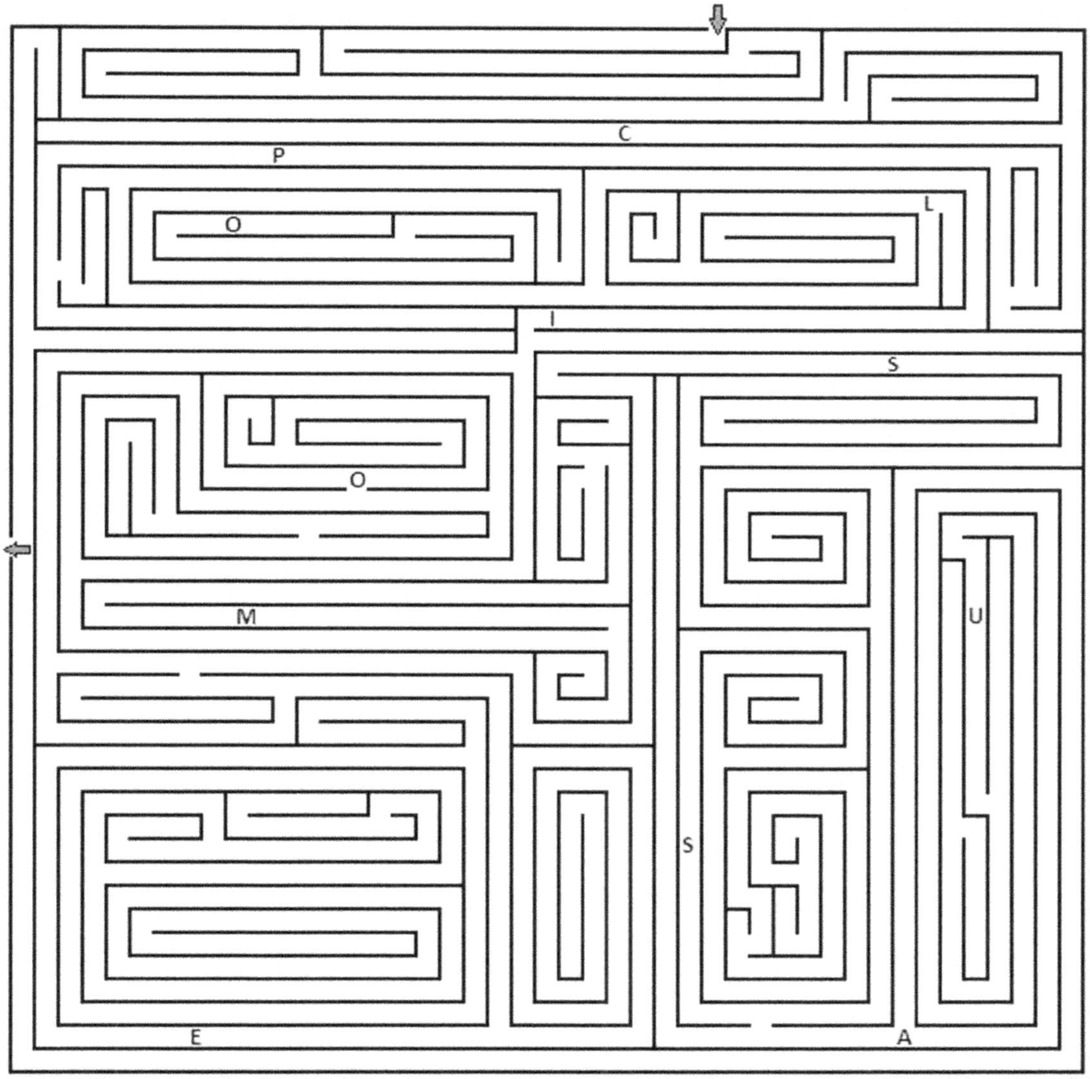

Rome - Points of Interest

Milan - Points of Interest

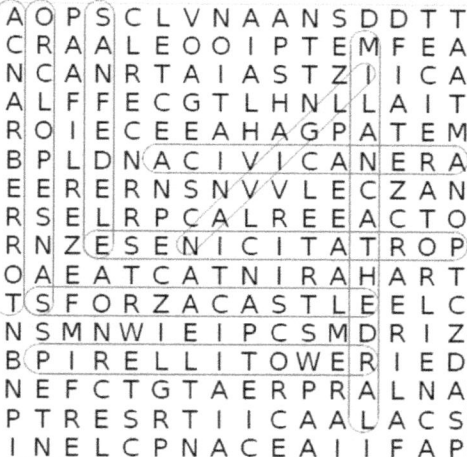

Crossword

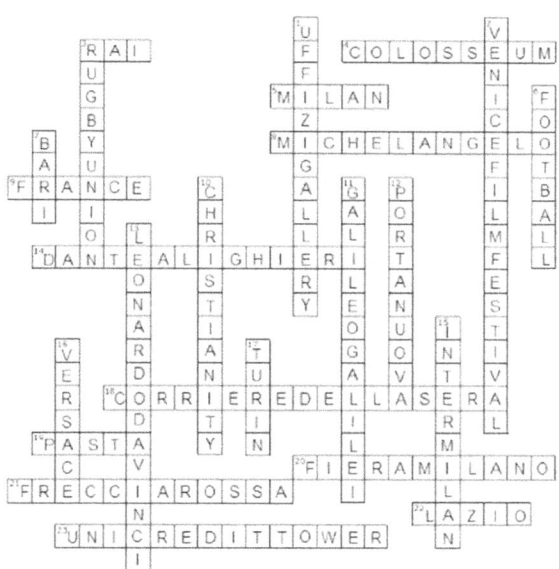

Maze

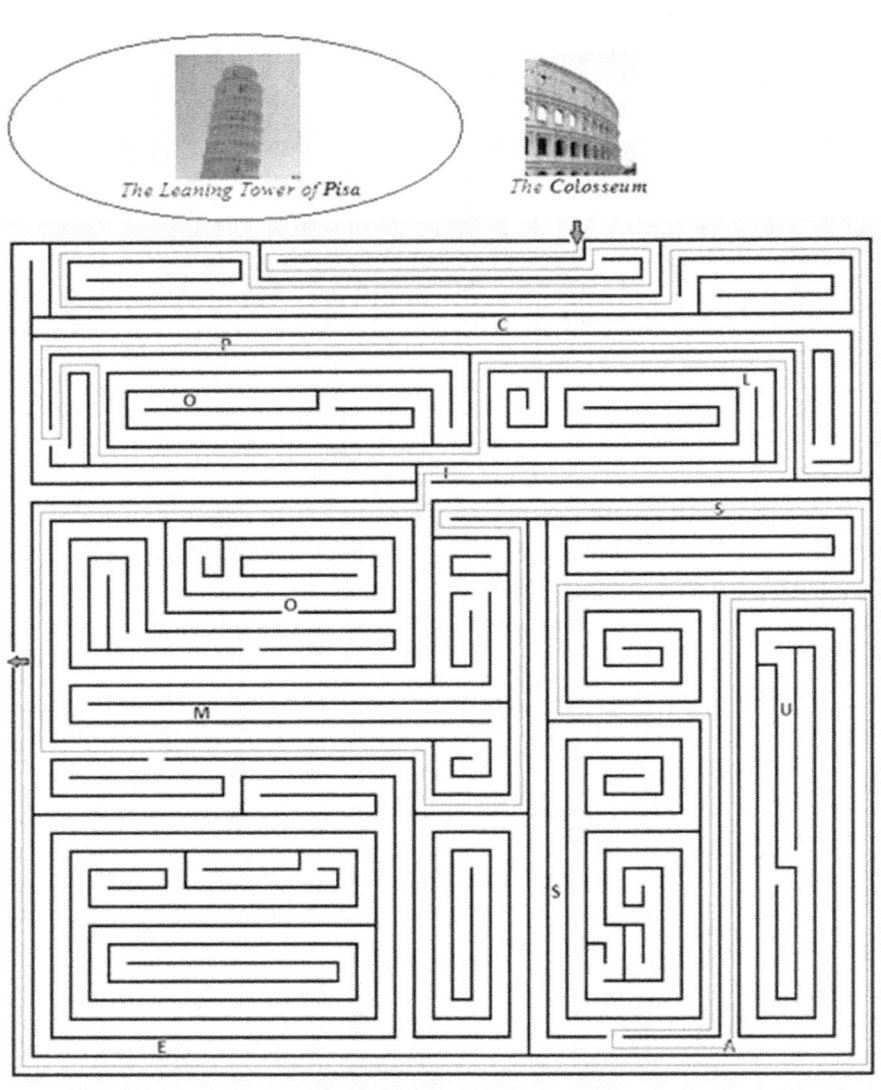

The Leaning Tower of Pisa

The Colosseum